The First Flame

Hannah Hagie

BookLeaf Publishing

India | USA | UK

Presentation by *BookLeaf Publishing*

Web: www.bookleafpub.com

E-mail: info@bookleafpub.com

ISBN: 9789363300705

First edition 2024

To my mother. With love.

ACKNOWLEDGEMENT

Thank you to everyone working behind the scenes to make this poetry book become a reality. And thank you to every person supporting me as I start my writing journey. This is just the beginning.

Mama

Mama, please help me.
What if they don't like the words I write?

Mama, please help me.
I'm not strong enough for this fight.

Mama, please help me.
This isn't fun anymore.

Mama, please help me.
From my soul, the words pour.

Mama, please help me.
Just one last letter.

Mama, please help me.
Does it ever get better?

The Cut

I am not who I once was,
and how can I decide
whether that makes me better
or worse?

The growth of a lock
too long,
over twelve months
of ups and downs,
spinning dizzy
and debating
if I should make the cut.

Golds and coppers
cascading down my shoulders,
knotting together
like it controls what I do,
shrouding my vision
like it controls
what I see.

Who are you?
And I don't know.

How is it going?
And I still don't know.
I am not who I once was.

I can almost taste
the freedom
of being right
where I want to be,
but not knowing how
to achieve
the change I know I should make.

Maybe just one simple cut,
not exactly a loss of length,
but a gain
of the person who
I know I once was.
Who I know I can be.

The Flame

A spark.
Small at first,
ignited by breath,
then roaring with light.

Inhale.
The burn.
The disgust.
The poison.

Exhale.
One, two,
three.

Nothing but a cry for help
left unanswered
as it wafts through the air.
Nothing but a hazy cloud
as it envelops the soul.

Inhale.
It does not subside,
this burn that grows
with each breath of life.

Exhale.
The walls are falling
down.
The roof is
caving in.

One puff.
Two.

A flick.
A soul of a shoe
as it snuffs out the flame,
discards of the poison.

Exhale.
Grasping
for the comfort
as it disperses in the wind.
Leaving the scene
as the butt lays smoldering
in the
distance.

And the flame
is forgotten,
but the addiction
stays
within reason.

A Secret I Can't Keep

Dwelling on a moment,
a secret that I know of.
An obsession so strong
over a fear
of the man's love.

An addiction so
yearned for.
He only wants
more.
It's taking all I've got
not to run
out the back door.

And the child knows nothing
between wrongs and rights.
But one day, the fury
will turn into spite.

And I carry it with me,
a secret I can't keep.
One that grows in time,
that could break more hearts
than mine,
but one day, the wounds
he will reap.

A secret I cannot speak of.
Please make it
go away.
I'm not sure how much longer
my silence will remain.

Karma

What they don't know
won't hurt them.
But what I do know
hurts me.

A whisper of a secret,
burning reputation,
breaking reality.

You can't tell them.
And they can't know.
Because what other choice
do you have
if you don't just leave it alone?

A permanent scar.
A juvenile lust.
A ghost of a presence
on skin it never should have touched.

And a look in the mirror,
a smile on your face.
What they don't know
won't hurt them,
but only one can win
the race.

Death of a Poet

9

Let's watch as the storm
rips its way through the town.
And our very last hopes are
blown away by the clouds.

It's no use.
We'll never survive.
Turn and close the screen door.
Who cares if I rhyme?

I've Never Felt Grief

They say we all feel grief
in different ways.
But how can I understand that
when I haven't truly felt grief myself?

When I cannot sympathize with others
without feeling guilt that I have not
experienced something similar.

I shouldn't have to feel guilty
over lacking a loss.
But how can I say
"All my grandparents are alive,"
without feeling like I'm offending them.

I've never lost a lifelong family pet,
but my beloved hamster died
when I was sixteen. And years later,
I discovered that hamsters hibernate
and maybe I buried him alive.

I've never lost a grandparent,
but my dad's adopted father died of cancer,
and I refused to give the man one last hug
good-bye,
because I was six years old
and thought he smelled bad.

What is grief
if I have not felt it?
Or
have I?

I've never lost a sibling,
but my friend's little sister
just died in a car accident,
and I've been stunned to silence
for the past twelve hours.

And maybe I have felt grief,
but not in the ways I thought I would.
And maybe I haven't felt my own grief,
but I have felt others'.

When the car accident happened.
When a girl I went to school with
died from a drunk driver
on that same road.

I've never felt grief,
but I know people who have.
And I know one day,
I will feel a grief much larger
than my dead hamster,
and I will wish this poem
was still my reality.

A Pawn in the Controversy

I don't know how
to combat these flames.
I'm afraid that nothing
will remain the same.

They say love thy neighbor,
but it's quite a shame
that I'm living in a country
of hate and blame.

One wrong move.
One wrong belief.
Two differing sides
can't even make peace.

And this system is a joke,
existing only for
supremacy.
And I'm left in doubt
if these people
truly love our country.

And they turn us
against each other
to hide the changes
being made undercover.

Adding fuel to the fight
between red and blue,
we are no longer one country,
but one split in two.

The Truth Is

The truth is,
I hate
living
in this
mess.

The truth is,
it's so
hard
to keep
my mouth
shut.

The truth is,
nobody
will
open
their eyes
and see.

The truth is,
I feel
doomed.

The truth is,
we are

all
doomed.

The truth is,
I'm scared
of the bumps
in the road.

The truth is,
I stopped
caring
a long
time
ago.

The Dirt

Ask him how it felt that day,
a river so impure.
And the cast now wrapped around
her soul, never to unfurl.
A print so dirty,
left behind
to ruin her entire world.
A blossom of pure innocence
hidden like a saltwater pearl.

Ask him about the words
he begged me not to say.
And every promise offered
never saw the light of day.
How if I'd only waited,
you'd be gone
and I'd take your place.
How every toxic memory
scarred more than just
her face.

Ask him where he was
that night you were away.
How she wished with everything in her
that he was there to stay.
A secret bestowed
during the trance,

a single missed call
and she lost her chance.
And a scarlet silhouette
shakes its head
and drowns in her regret.

Ask him how it feels
now, looking at
her progress.
How he's not even
a thought left
drifting through her
conscience.
How he'll never
find happiness
in the size of his ego.
And how moving forward
is now her favorite
vertigo.

Ask him what he'd do
if she hauled it from behind,
put on display like Barbies
as she uncovers
every lie.
And his filthy little secrets
could be exposed so soon,
but the dirt dug up
could end in more
than his own doom.

Beauty

I want to write
about beauty.

But not just the
stereotypical
beauty.

But the type of beauty
in a lavender-
filled, setting
sky.

The type of beauty
while standing
in the middle of
a greenhouse.

The type of beauty
in a bouquet
of fresh-cut
flowers.

The type of beauty
in a vine-ripened
tomato.

The type of beauty
in baking
homemade bread.

Why have we made
a stigma
out of beauty in
ourselves?

In the eyes.
In the hair.
In the body.

Beauty
is more than
us.

It is what is
all around us.

It is what we
cannot
control.

And I would
fight a thousand
battles
to show
the entire world.

I Like

I like the softness
in your smiles,
and the way
your hair curls.
And the protection
that you offer,
and the tightness
of your holds.

I like how
you make me better,
and the ambition
behind your eyes.
And the strength
that you bring me,
and how it never dies.

I like the image
of a future,
how there's so much
left in store.
How every little memory
I cherish even more.

And I like the way our love
is similar to no other.

How they don't have to
understand just how
we work together.

Euphoria

22

Outside
under the warm sun
where I lay.
A healing
so euphoric
it cannot
be replaced.
Pulling me down
into the Earth
below.
I am the child
of a calm, sunny
glow.
A force so deep
and no song left
unsung.
They will no longer
deplete us of the life
we wanted all along.

Another World

As if the only good place
in this world
is in the palms of nature,
where not a single leaf
is left unsettled.

A dream of a land
so far from the near future,
another strand of hope to get us
to tomorrow.

A powerful force, blushing and sharp-
and in the hands of its creator,
it will prosper.

Another day of crafting
the beauty so
commonly sought-for.

Another imagination
pulled taut at the seams.

And a final rustle
of the lungs
as the winning breath
is redeemed.

Rosemary

Rosemary,
you found yourself
far away,
too far gone to
remember how to play.

There's a blur
in the eye
from your life
flashing by.
But you'll know
what to do
in the morning.

Rosemary,
stop and smell the roses.
You're too young to know
where you're going.

And you wish
with all your might,
that it may still
be alright.

Around the sunny side
of the bustling creek,

where old dreams come
to drown in peace.

And you know
when the time comes,
all will be
better.

But you don't rush the things
that are taking their time
to get here.

The Sweetest Soul

A thousand aches
and a curse at who
I doubt in.
The sweetest soul
now lost in the deep end.

And there is no humor
in the ferocity of the virus,
in the inevitability of the end.

A land once so grand,
but it is often that the gloom
shines mightier than the sun.

There is no pause and no break,
only meaningless prayers that
build hope and shatter it all the same.

Finish Line

I walk this road
a million times,
and somehow I'm worried
there is nothing left
to find.
But with every beat,
every lap,
and every deep breath,
the strength I have
pushes me further
down the path.
A little leap
of progress,
a goal set close
to view,
and the branches we broke
mean nothing
if the bridge doesn't
fall down too.

When I Think of You

When I think of you,
I think of how you hold me,
snug against your chest,
feeling as if I'm protected
by the force of the strongest army.

When I think of you,
I think of your warmth, and how
it envelops me like the quilt
we so often share.
I think of your scent, and how
every inhale of it takes me home,
how the faintest trace of it
left on my clothing
reminds me of how much of you
I have.

When I think of you,
I think of how refreshing it feels
to never feel doubt or
question my role. To have
love reciprocated and not
just stolen.

I think of
how safe I feel

knowing that it's
genuine.
How I can love you
without fear
that it will hurt one day
too.
How I cannot fathom
the idea of loving
anyone but you.

Older

When I was younger,
and the world felt so free,
like how I had the chance
at any opportunity.
And I could enjoy
the little things,
like playing in the mud,
or learning how to braid,
only knowing love.

When I was older,
and the pictures
turned out clearer.
A bouquet of
innocence
wilted by
the bearer.
A pretty picture
tainted by the
opaqueness of the shade,
and youth taken advantage of
seldom did remain.

And I'm older now,
and it's

so
hard
to find the light
in a world
slowly falling
a p a r t.

But if we give up,
what will be left?
No more land,
no more plants,
no more life,
no more death?

And I'm old,
and I know that
surrender is out of reach.
That it's actually us
who are destined to teach.
And a new light is shining
down the hallway
we'd forgotten.
There is still hope
for life that enjoys
what they've gotten.

Homestretch

Seamless are the edges
in which I write my words.
Scratched out in the margins,
where all my doubt unfurls.
And I fail
every time
that I hit the backspace
or erase a letter.
But my words are like magic,
only one has the power
to muster.
And I try the pencil again,
not forgetting
where I've been.
Retired stories,
forgotten verses,
and characters missing
their happy-ends.
In comes the tide
that pulls me to the letters,
that scratches every motivation
lingering in the shadows.
And ahead is the final page,
the few words I must write-
from there the story ends,
from there I wrote it right.

Twenty and One

Stop.
See me in a different color.
I'm sitting here
waiting
for the world
to get better.

Learn from a single story,
pages turned in reflection,
a pen's stroke
is the guide
to utmost perfection.

I am weightless,
far gone in a world
of my own.
Where I prosper
and enjoy
a life
that I've earned.

I make no apologies
for the words
I have written.
In fact, only I

know the truths
I have hidden.

Radical doses,
mediocre moments,
a flask full of happiness,
and a silence unbroken.

I am not who I once was.
Instead, I am better.
Who are they to drag me down?
Who am I to forget her?

I conjured hope
in a thousand
broken hearts.
Put the pieces
back together
and created
my art.

This long road ahead
may not always
seem possible.
But with my words
and my heart,
I strive to be unstoppable.

www.ingramcontent.com/pod-product-compliance
Lightning Source LLC
LaVergne TN
LVHW010931200726

843509LV00013B/2161